DESIGN THINKING

BOOKS IN THE LIBRARY FUTURES SERIES

ALA✿
Neal-Schuman
CHICAGO | 2020

ALA CENTER FOR THE FUTURE OF LIBRARIES

DESIGN THINKING

RACHEL IVY CLARKE

LIBRARY FUTURES ④

RACHEL IVY CLARKE is an assistant professor at Syracuse University's School of Information Studies. Her research focuses on the application of design methodologies and epistemologies to librarianship in order to facilitate the systematic, purposeful design of library services and library education. Her current projects include the IMLS-funded Designing Future Library Leaders project, which is investigating the integration of design methods and principles in graduate-level library education, and the OCLC/ALISE-funded project The Critical Catalog, which draws on critical design methodology to provoke the exploration of diverse library reading materials. Clarke holds a BA in creative writing from California State University, Long Beach, an MLIS from San Jose State University, and a PhD from the University of Washington. Her dissertation, which argues that the field of librarianship is more appropriately viewed as a design field rather than a scientific one, received the 2017 iSchools dissertation award and the 2018 ALISE/Eugene Garfield dissertation award.

ISBNs
978-0-8389-1792-3 (paper)
978-0-8389-4687-9 (ePub)
978-0-8389-4688-6 (PDF)
978-0-8389-4689-3 (Kindle)

Library of Congress Control Number: 2019040310

Cover design by Kimberly Thornton. Composition by Alejandra Diaz in the Adobe Garamond Pro, Vista Sans and Vista Slab typefaces.

♾ This paper meets the requirements of ANSI/NISO Z39.48-1992 (Permanence of Paper).

Printed in the United States of America
24   23   22   21   20   5   4   3   2   1

ALA Neal-Schuman purchases fund advocacy, awareness, and accreditation programs for library professionals worldwide.

CONTENTS

FOREWORD

BY MIGUEL A. FIGUEROA

Center for the Future of Libraries
American Library Association

WHAT IF OUR DISCIPLINE MADE THE SHIFT FROM A SCIENCE approach (organizing our professional knowledge in the form of testable explanations and predictions about the world) toward a design approach (identifying problems and addressing them with human-centered solutions)? It is a subtle shift, but in many ways it is reflected in the ways that more and more of our organizations are moving, engaging with their communities, testing solutions, involving users in the evaluation of those solutions, and readapting to the greatest purpose and outcome for the information needed.

For the past several years, Dr. Rachel Ivy Clarke has been at the forefront of reimagining a library profession focused on design. Her work has shown how library leaders, past and present, have leveraged the tools of design. She has advocated for a more deliberate use of design as critical to advancing the profession, especially at a time when the artificial barriers and hierarchies between our institutions and communities are vanishing. In *Design Thinking*, Clarke succinctly demonstrates why libraries' futures should be both curious about and involved with the world's fascination with design.

Fighting off the idea that *design thinking* is just the latest buzz word in startup culture or education, Clarke grounds her approach in a recognition that design thinking is a way and process of thinking that has been used throughout history, both in and out of libraries, as part of society's and culture's evolution. What has changed since the 1960s and has become more apparent in the last decade is the formalization of and focus on design thinking as a process that can be practiced, applied, and adapted across sectors. Through this progression, design thinking has become a popular tool for thinking and doing that is oriented toward human-centered problem solving. As Clarke summarizes, this process inevitably includes some forms of empathetic discovery, problem definition, idea generation, creation, and then evaluation, which can cycle problem solvers back into any one of the previous steps.

How does this process translate into librarianship? Here again, in "Design Thinking from the Field," Clarke makes the case that our profession has evolved because library staff—intentionally or instinctively—leveraged a process like design thinking to better meet the needs of communities. From the creation of *Poole's Index* in the mid-1800s, to the introduction of the book wagon and modern outreach services in the early 1900s, to the creation and popularization of "tough topics" handouts in just this past decade, library workers have designed solutions for information problems. As design thinking has been formalized and entered the mainstream, more libraries have integrated the process into their designs of physical spaces, signage, and wayfinding; their outreach to specific populations; and even their improvements of the library catalog.

How do we move from the occasional integration of design to realizing more intentional roles as information and library designers? In "For the Future," Clarke encourages readers to pursue three paths—understanding and applying elements from the larger context of design, moving from human-centered to values-centered design, and including design explicitly in library education and in workplace cultures. She encourages libraries to go further with design, integrating critique and reflection as tools to maintain our responsibility to the communities that we serve. Looking at our profession (distinct from a trade or industry), Clarke recognizes that library design cannot simply be responsive to the passing popular wants of our communities—it must embrace our more timeless commitments to values. By bringing broader elements of design and making into our professional values, we make design more of our own. That acknowledgement and ownership of design will be solidified by integrating design principles into educational preparation for professionals and purposeful changes to our organizations (libraries, systems, agencies, and associations) to build solutions for the problems we all face.

Design thinking echoes many of the movements happening in libraries. And while it is a loaded term for some people, design thinking, as Clarke presents it here, is an approach that we can all appreciate and learn from.

UNDERSTANDING DESIGN THINKING

THE PHRASE *DESIGN THINKING* **MAY SEEM LIKE A** new buzzword that's all the rage in our current world. But despite recent popular applications, design thinking is not a new concept: it is a way of thinking as old as humans themselves. For as long as human beings have been making things, they have been designing. Everything from the earliest stone axes to today's iPhones are products of design; that is, a process of creation with the intent of solving problems.

Those who only see the end results of this process—the axe or the iPhone—may take these acts of creation for granted. Since we don't often see the work that goes into designing these products, we may think the design process is simple, easy, or is even a magical feat that only people born with certain talents can pull off. But just because we don't see the work of designing doesn't mean it's not there. All skilled professionals make their work look easy, from a basketball player gracefully sinking a basket to an actor seamlessly transitioning into an entirely different character. Even librarians make professional services like database-searching and readers' advisory seem like magic to people not trained in those skills. Design also requires the same amount of hard work, training, and practice to achieve a level of proficiency where the results appear magical.

Although this kind of design work has been occurring throughout human history, it is only in the second half of the twentieth century that scholars have looked at *how* this "magical" work occurs—the methods, processes, and perspectives that designers undertake to create products. It is out of this movement that the phrase *design thinking* emerged.

A BRIEF HISTORY

The phrase *design thinking* originated in the 1960s. Herbert Simon first proposed that design constitutes a unique way of thinking that is different from traditional scientific ways of thinking,[1] but L. Bruce Archer is generally recognized as the first person to use the phrase *design thinking* to describe this alternative mindset.[2] Archer and numerous other researchers and theorists, including Bryan Lawson,[3] Peter G. Rowe,[4] and Nigel Cross,[5] spent a great deal of time studying designers across various settings—architecture, fashion design, graphic design, engineering, software development, and more—to understand both the thought processes and actions that underlie design work. Thus "design thinking" refers equally to what designers are *thinking* while they work in addition to what they are *doing* while they work. Many of these scholars were

---

1. Herbert Simon, *The Sciences of the Artificial* (Cambridge, MA: MIT Press, 1969).
2. L. Bruce Archer, *Systematic Method for Designers* (Council of Industrial Design, H.M.S.O., 1965).
3. Bryan Lawson, *How Designers Think: The Design Process Demystified* (London: Architectural, 1980).
4. Peter G. Rowe, *Design Thinking* (Cambridge, MA: MIT Press, 1987).
5. Nigel Cross, "Designerly Ways of Knowing," *Design Studies* 3, no. 4 (1982): 221–27; Nigel Cross, *Design Thinking: Understanding How Designers Think and Work* (Oxford: Berg, 2011).

especially interested in understanding not just how designers create, but how they create good, innovative designs. Again and again, they found that designers work—and think about their work—in unique ways.

As with most jobs, working designers engage in this creative mindset and process automatically—design thinking is not something they consider while they're working, it's just what they do. But the scholarship that surfaced the concept of design thinking has enabled designers to become more intentional about their design processes, and to purposefully apply elements of designerly ways of working and thinking. One famous example is IDEO. Founded in 1991, IDEO began as a traditional design firm focused on designing consumer products like toothbrushes and chairs.[6] One thing that set IDEO apart from other design firms, however, was its intentional focus on the process of design: what were designers doing and why? This led to new mindsets, like the idea that users' reactions to design products could never be predicted, no matter how much user research the designers had conducted; and it also led to new processes, like using rapid, disposable prototypes to test and modify ideas quickly in response to user feedback. IDEO demonstrated its new approach by designing a new grocery market shopping cart in a 1999 episode of *Nightline*. This exposed a whole new non-design audience to the principles and processes of design thinking. David Kelley, one of IDEO's founders, found it challenging to explain this new design approach to people, so he drew on the phrase *design thinking* to explain it.[7] Although the phrase already existed, it is arguably Kelley's use of the term that brought the term into popular culture.

---

6. Tim Brown and Jocelyn Wyatt, "Design Thinking for Social Innovation," *Stanford Social Innovation Review*, Winter 2010, https://ssir.org/articles/entry/design_thinking_for _social_innovation.

7. Tim Brown, *Change by Design: How Design Thinking Transforms Organizations and Inspires Innovation* (New York: Harper Business, 2009).

Design thinking has gone on to be used in a variety of settings outside of traditional design work. By 2001, IDEO was increasingly engaging in projects that were outside the scope of traditional product design. Instead of designing more ergonomic chairs or more efficient shopping carts, IDEO found itself tackling less tangible outcomes, such as restructuring the organization of a health care foundation, helping a 100-year-old manufacturing company better understand its clients, and creating alternative school learning environments beyond traditional classrooms. This type of work took IDEO from designing consumer products to "designing consumer experiences"[8] and demonstrated that design products extend beyond tangible, physical things. Other organizations have recognized this shift in design from a focus on the looks and usability of physical products to intangible experiences. Businesses such as Proctor and Gamble, Kaiser Permanente, and Costco have applied design thinking to their strategic planning, business models, and organizational structures and processes. Prominent books like Tim Brown and Barry Katz's *Change by Design: How Design Thinking Transforms Organizations and Inspires Innovation* (2009) and Roger Martin's *The Design of Business: Why Design Thinking Is the Next Competitive Advantage* (2009) have argued for the application of design thinking in corporate environments, especially in management and leadership. Those organizations that have embraced design thinking and methods have been shown to do better financially than their less design-conscious competitors. In addition to corporations, design thinking is increasingly being applied to work toward the greater social good in settings like health care, charitable foundations, social innovation start-ups, national governments, and elementary schools. Education is needed to

---

8. Brown and Wyatt, "Design Thinking for Social Innovation."

support these wider applications of design thinking, and this need has inspired programs like Stanford University's Hasso Plattner Institute of Design. Founded by David Kelley and affectionately referred to as the "d.school," the Plattner Institute helped to popularize some of IDEO's design thinking approaches. Other schools and universities are now including design thinking as a pedagogical focus, either through formal degree programs in design thinking, such as the one at Radford University, or by pervasive application throughout the curriculum, such as at Smith College. In the contemporary world, design thinking no longer denotes just the aesthetics or usability of a physical product—it's a worldwide movement rooted in a creative mindset.

THE DESIGN THINKING MINDSET

The phrase *design thinking* is used to describe two different but overlapping concepts:

1. A unique way of looking at the world, and
2. A process of activities and methods that reflect and support that worldview.

The worldview or mindset helps you carry out the process, and the process helps people discover and harness the mindset. Let's talk first about the overarching themes of the design thinking mindset, and then dive into how they are applied in the design thinking process.

Design thinking is a unique way of thinking about the world. The fundamental difference between design thinking and other mindsets is its focus on *problem solving*. It might seem at first that other worldviews also focus on problem solving. For instance, it might seem that scientific ways of thinking, such as the scientific method, target problem solving:

for example, how scientific discoveries can help solve the problem of air pollution. However, science is focused on observing and understanding with the intent of making predictions about the natural world. Science helps us understand that we have a problem with air pollution and that the problem is likely to get worse over time. Such scientific findings can contribute to problem solving, perhaps by inspiring smog regulations for vehicles. But this problem solving is a secondary outcome when compared to the attainment of predictive knowledge. Design, on the other hand, intentionally targets problem solving. The mindset of design thinking always has problem solving at its heart.

What kinds of problems does design thinking solve? Design thinking can be used to address any problem that needs a creative solution. Although traditional applications of design may have focused on aesthetic or usability problems, design is not limited to solving problems about how to make a product more visually appealing or a service easier to navigate. In fact, design is especially well-suited to solving what are known as "wicked problems"; these are unique, interconnected, and poorly defined problems that cannot be definitively described. Horst Rittel and Melvin Webber, the generators of the idea of wicked problems, suggest ten characteristics that identify a problem as "wicked" (see figure 1).

Reducing air pollution is a great example of a wicked problem. Although the term *air pollution* may have a specific connotation, it's actually not one single problem, since air pollution may stem from a variety of sources. There are various ways of addressing the problem of air pollution, ranging from government-imposed regulations, to consumer education, to the development of new technologies that support low- or non-emissions vehicles. None of these proposed solutions are correct or incorrect, but some may be better or worse depending on the context in which they are set. There is no complete, articulated set of steps that will always work to solve the problem of air pollution, and

FIGURE 1 ——————————————————————————————————————
Rittel and Webber's ten characteristics of wicked problems (1973)

1	There is no definitive problem or known solution.
2	The problem has no stopping rule.
3	There are no true or false solutions to the problem, only good or bad solutions.
4	No scientific test exists for a solution.
5	Each solution is a "one shot" effort (that is, every solution attempt changes the problem).
6	There is no complete list of acceptable moves.
7	The problem is unique.
8	The solution is a symptom of another problem.
9	There is more than one explanation or framing for the problem.
10	The designer is liable for the actions they take in attempting a solution.

any step we take to work towards a solution will add new elements and characteristics that change the problem and reveal additional problems. Because these "wicked problems" cannot be solved through traditional scientific means and may only have better or worse resolutions rather than a single "correct" answer, creative approaches like design are necessary. Design is often relied upon to tackle wicked problems that have failed to be solved via more traditional research approaches.

If wicked problems are so hard to define and articulate, how can we even begin to approach them? In addition to problem solving, design also relies on *problem finding* and *problem framing*. First, we have to understand what the problem really is. Is the problem really air pollution, or is air pollution merely a symptom of another problem? Designers use investigative research and other methods and techniques to identify the *real* problem that needs to be addressed. Many designers claim that it is just as important—if not more important—to identify and define a problem than it is to solve it, since any suggested solution stems from the definition of the problem. Designers also define problems by adding boundaries and constraints. In the air pollution example, there might be set boundaries of scope, such as geographic region. Or there might be constraints in terms of resources like knowledge or money. Designers also reframe problems—that is, they look at them from another angle or point of view. Research about how designers work found that the ability to reframe or refit problems was common across fields like industrial product design, software and technology development, and architecture. Reframing can be as simple as looking at air pollution from an individual perspective (i.e., what a single person can do in their daily life to help reduce air pollution) rather than an organizational perspective.

If the goal of design thinking is to solve problems, then the outcome is the *creation* of some kind of solution. Often we assume that these creations will be physical products like chairs, toothbrushes, smartphones, and buildings. But design is not just about physical products. Creations can also be digital, like websites, apps, or software; or even intangible intellectual constructs like curricula, policies, procedures, and processes. Experiences are also designed to address problems, which is why we find so much overlap between design thinking and the user experience (UX) field. Anything created by people to solve problems is design.

Even though design can create intangible solutions, these are almost always represented and communicated in some tangible form. Policies are recorded in documents; user experiences may be described with photographs, maps, signage, videos, and so on. Making ideas tangible and concrete helps the creative process and facilitates communication.[9]

---

9. Hasso Plattner, Christoph Meinel, and Larry Leifer, *Design Thinking: Understand, Improve, Apply* (Heidelberg: Springer, 2011).

Working with tangible materials, even for intangible products, may inspire new ideas or help designers consider new constraints that could affect the situation. Nowhere is this more evident than in the maker movement, and especially its applications in education, where the physical construction of an object helps people learn new concepts and think more concretely and critically.

While there are many possible approaches to problem solving and creation in the broader discipline of design, design thinking explicitly takes a *human-centered* approach. Design thinking stems from the perspective that all design activity is social in nature, therefore humans must be at the center of the process. This means that people are the focus of any problem to be addressed. Compare this, for example, with system-centered design, an approach that focuses on the functional capability of a product. A major influence on the shift from system-centered approaches to a focus on the users of a system can be traced to Donald Norman's book *The Design of Everyday Things* (2013, revised edition). Norman emphasized that a design should be focused on the needs of the people who will use it, rather than solely on functionality or aesthetics—a revolutionary perspective at the time.

While design thinking certainly focuses on users by putting their needs first and foremost when creating solutions, being user-centered is not necessarily exactly the same as being human-centered. Jeanne Liedtka, Randy Salzman, and Daisy Azer, authors of *Design Thinking for the Greater Good* (2017), note that to be human-centered means to start with real people, not demographic profiles or market segments.[10] Instead of relying on nameless and faceless statistics and descriptions, design thinking requires deep explorations into people's lives before beginning to generate solutions. Empathy—as opposed to knowledge alone—is key.

---

10. Jeanne Liedtka, Randy Salzman, and Daisy Azer, *Design Thinking for the Greater Good: Innovation in the Social Sector* (New York, NY: Columbia University Press, 2017).

Another key component of design thinking is *divergent thinking*. This is a thought process used to generate creative ideas through the exploration of many possible solutions. The basic idea here is that instead of converging on a single idea or solution, we should generate as many ideas as possible in order to expand our potential creativity. Because design thinking emphasizes multiple approaches to solving a problem, it generates more—and more innovative—solutions. This focus on quantity over quality helps ensure that diverse options are explored and that a designer does not narrow in on one solution preemptively or close off additional possibilities too soon. (See figure 2.)

Divergent thinking often occurs in a spontaneous, free-flowing, nonlinear way in which the generation of one idea leads to another, and the juxtaposition of multiple ideas leads to unexpected connections that foster even more new ideas. While it sometimes seems like divergent thinking comes more naturally to some people than others, we should remember that no one is born with magical design skills; they just make it look easy because they've been doing it for a long time. The longer a designer has worked, the more experiences and examples they have in their repertoire to draw on. A designer may start by riffing on preexisting designs, or juxtaposing multiple designs to inspire new ideas. Collaboration with others is also a good way to foster divergent thinking. Sure, the old saying that "two heads are better than one" is a cliché, but a combination of people of diverse backgrounds and perspectives will certainly be able to offer more suggestions than one single perspective alone. IDEO is well-known not just for emphasizing collaborative teamwork, but for intentionally building teams of people from different backgrounds. For example, the team tasked with designing a new shopping cart included an engineer, a Harvard MBA, a linguist, a marketing expert, a psychologist, and an undergraduate biology major.

To generate an abundance of ideas, design thinking also relies on the premise that *anything is possible*. This means that in addition to having a broad repertoire, designers also need a powerful imagination, and an ability to relax or even ignore existing constraints. If you're trying to come up with new and innovative ideas, but you constantly have to worry about them being too expensive or otherwise impossible to implement, it's unlikely that you'll be able to come up with anything

FIGURE 2 ———————————————————————————

A model of divergent thinking

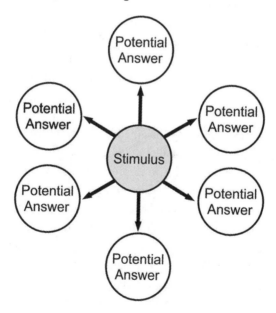

By Aishwarya.gudadhe – Own work, CC BY-SA 4.0 (https://creativecommons.org/licenses/by -sa/4.0/), https://commons.wikimedia.org/w/index.php?curid=41263671, image has been cropped.

innovative at all. Of course, costs and other constraints are a concern—but thinking about them too early will curtail innovative ideas. When generating ideas, a designer probably won't have all the answers about how that design will be created or how much it will cost, so a certain amount of comfort with ambiguity is necessary.

Given the number of possible solution ideas for any design problem, not all of them will be good ideas—and that's okay! Designers are *comfortable with failure*, because they are not hung up on one single proposed solution. If you're afraid to fail, it's also likely that you're afraid to deviate from the status quo, which impedes innovation. Being okay with failure is part of what allows designers not just to generate large numbers of imaginative ideas, but also to take risks and propose crazy solutions that might lead to innovative products and services. Although this is one of the most important aspects of the design mindset, it is also one of the most invisible, since end users only see finished items, not all of the failed trial and error that went into creating that final product or service.

In addition to supporting imaginative and innovative ideas, being comfortable with failure also allows designers to learn from their mistakes and use that knowledge to improve their designs. Therefore, a key tenet of design thinking is *iteration*. Iteration literally means repetition: doing something over and over again, while making progressive improvements to the design. With design thinking, it means having the perspective that no product or service is ever completely finished: it can always be improved. Some designers even say that "all design is redesign." Approaching problems iteratively lets designers be open to alteration and change if something seems wrong or is not working. An iterative mindset allows for reflection, refinement over time, and continual improvement of a design in response to previous results and new or evolving information, knowledge, and situations. The iterative mindset is especially relevant when tackling wicked problems, which always generate or reveal new problems during the creation of a solution.

THE DESIGN THINKING PROCESS

Design thinking is a way of thinking—it's a way of looking at the world that is guided by problem finding, framing, and solving; creativity; human-centeredness; divergent thinking; the idea that anything is possible; comfort with failure; and iteration. But the phrase *design thinking* is also used to refer to a process model that reflects this worldview. In the most basic sense, the process consists of defining a problem and then creating and implementing a solution. But there are lots of models and processes in the world that can be used to solve problems. What separates the design thinking process from these other approaches is the movement through multiple phases that are grounded in the main tenets of the design way of thinking.

These phases have been outlined by various major design firms and sources of design thinking instruction. While the phases in each of these sources can be given various names or grouped and organized differently, it's easy to see clear commonalities among them (see figure 3).

Despite variations, we can see a pattern emerge. The design thinking process consists of the following:

1. Some kind of empathetic discovery
2. Some kind of problem definition
3. Some kind of idea generation
4. Some kind of creation
5. Some kind of evaluation

You cannot solve a problem if you don't know what problems exist. Therefore, the first phase of the design thinking process starts with *empathetic discovery*—finding out exactly what is going on in a given space or context. This stage of the process establishes a problem solving mindset by identifying patterns, and clearly articulating issues and goals through human-centered techniques that emphasize an empathetic understanding of users and customers by seeing things from their perspective. Although they often make it look easy, designers don't just magically know how to empathize with users. Designers have many tools and methods they use to gain understanding and insight. One self-described "toolbox" of service design methods offers twenty-five different methods that service designers utilize to understand users, from fairly well-known strategies like personas, shadowing, and role-playing to innovative methods like expectation maps, mobile ethnography, and "service safaris." While there are potentially an unlimited number of methods, the one common factor is that they all focus on thoroughly understanding the user. Empathetic understanding of users is key to understanding and framing problems.

Only when you really understand what it is like to be a user can you *identify and define specific problems* that can be tackled. If you don't fully understand the user, you risk making assumptions about what problems exist, and you may jump too quickly to generate solutions that turn out to miss the mark. In this phase, designers take all of the information gleaned in the discovery phase and use it to identify specific issues and problems faced by users. They look for patterns and common themes, but they also reflect on what it feels like to face a problem. They look for breakdowns in existing systems or tools or experience. Some people refer to these as "pain points"—difficulties users face when trying to accomplish a task or interact with a system or interface. Along with

FIGURE 3

Organization and names of phases in the design thinking process from various sources

	gather inspiration		generate ideas	make ideas tangible		share the story
Design Thinking for Educators (IDEO)[ii]	discovery	interpretation	ideation	experimentation	evolution	
Design Thinking for Libraries Toolkit[iii]	inspiration		ideation			implementation
Stanford d.school[iv]	empathize	define	ideate	prototype	test	
Henry Ford Learning Institute[v]	empathy	define	ideate	prototype	feedback & reflect	
Design Council Double Diamond[vi]	discovery	define		develop		deliver
Nielsen Norman Group[vii]	understand		explore		materialize	
	empathize	define	ideate	prototype	test	implement

*(Note: the first header row represents the **IDEO U design thinking course**[i], with phases: discovery, interpretation, ideation, experimentation, evolution.)*

i. https://www.ideou.com/pages/design-thinking
ii. https://designthinkingforeducators.com/design-thinking/
iii. http://designthinkingforlibraries.com/
iv. https://dschool.stanford.edu/resources-collections/a-virtual-crash-course-in-design-thinking
v. https://hfli.org/design-thinking-workshops-press-release/
vi. https://www.designcouncil.org.uk/news-opinion/design-process-what-double-diamond
vii. https://www.nngroup.com/articles/design-thinking/

problem identification, a key component of this phase is definition. Merely finding a problem and saying "oh, there it is" is not enough. This is where designers use problem framing to set boundaries and scope and offer a particular angle or view on the problem that helps them drill down to specifics.

Next, designers *generate ideas.* This is a creative step that relies on divergent thinking to generate as many ideas for solutions as possible, no matter how absurd they may seem. Designers brainstorm tens, hundreds, sometimes thousands of ideas for potential solutions. No ideas are bad or wrong at this step. Designers embrace the mindset of possibility, and imagine new, futuristic solutions by asking "what if?" This phase can use a variety of techniques to foster divergent and imaginative thinking. Designers can look for ideas in other contexts: business, technology, television and other media, art, Internet culture, nature, and other cultures, societies, and countries. Some methods, like keeping a journal or sketchbook, or freewriting, may be done alone. Others, like brainstorming or mind-mapping, can be done in collaboration with others to generate even more ideas. In this phase, no idea is too big, too crazy, or too impossible. Even though we may know from the outset that some ideas are not feasible, we want to generate them anyway, since sometimes the strangest, most impossible ideas can inspire other, more realistic ones. Ideas can be generated in a variety of forms. Traditional design fields, like architecture and product design, rely on sketches and other quick, expressive—and most importantly, disposable—visual representations, like something you might find jotted on a cocktail napkin. As some ideas for design products reflect more intangible solutions, visual sketches may not sufficiently capture such ideas. Instead, these "sketches" might consist of a few words, some names, some arrows, whatever it takes to convey the general idea quickly and without involved investment. This kind of quick sketching encourages the numerous ideas needed for brainstorming. And the transitory and ephemeral nature of sketches makes them inherently disposable: no one feels bad if the sketch is discarded, because they didn't invest much time, money, or personnel in it.

As ideas become more fully formed, sketches evolve into more fully formed *creations*, although the line between the two can often be gray. This phase often involves *creating prototypes*, or low-fidelity preliminary mockups to test ideas and gather more feedback before committing to full development. Prototyping is often associated with shiny new revolutionary devices, often technological in nature. But the stereotypical conception of the shiny new prototype is actually counter to the purpose of prototyping.

A prototype doesn't have to be shiny, new, or finished—it is simply the first iteration of whatever you're designing. This phase takes ideas generated in the previous work and begins to manifest them in some kind of tangible form. A prototype doesn't have to be fully made. And it certainly doesn't have to be ready to implement or deploy. Heck, it doesn't even have to be real. It's better if prototypes are loose, informal, undetailed, and easy to generate. Maybe this sounds counterintuitive to designing a product or service that is eventually intended for actual implementation. But the more ideas you can prototype at a lower investment of time and resources, the more ideas you can try out and test. Paper prototyping is one very common design practice. When designing, say, a new web application or interface, designers go through many rounds of paper mockups and wireframes before writing a single line of computer code. While it may seem that a more realistic portrayal of the product would elicit more accurate user feedback, too much attention to detail can often be a setback, especially in the early stages of design.

Investing in full development too soon can hinder the refinement of a design product. The more details a mockup contains, the more the intended users will focus on those details, rather than on the overall design and whether or not it actually solves the problem. The prototype just has to reflect your design ideas enough to test and elicit feedback.

In the final phase the design product is shared, often with the intended users, with the explicit intention of *seeking feedback*. There are any number of methods and techniques that can be used in this phase, from interviewing potential users about a low-fidelity prototype to deploying a service and observing it in use. In addition to gleaning feedback about a design product's reception, this phase is also about improvement. Feedback about a design exposes new problems to be solved, either with a new iteration of the product or perhaps a new product idea entirely. While some may interpret this phase as the end of the design thinking process, the truth is that the design thinking process never ends. Design thinking is a cyclical, iterative process that allows for reflection on previous work and continual, ongoing improvement. While the entire process is cyclical, phases within the process may also be iterated. Designers are not obligated to follow this process in a linear fashion, but can (and often do) jump back and forth among these phases throughout their work. Perhaps a designer hits a snag during the protoyping phase that raises questions, raising the need for more in-depth user research. Prototypes often go through many rounds of feedback and refinement before a final product is deployed. This iterative mindset is core to the design thinking process.

DESIGN THINKING IN LIBRARIES

THE WAYS IN WHICH THE DESIGN THINKING MIND-set and process align with libraries seem obvious to me. For starters, libraries have always been rooted in *problem solving*. Think about it—what is a library itself but a solution to the problem of organizing and preserving knowledge for access by present and future generations? Libraries have addressed all manner of information problems, from chaining physical books to shelves in European monastic libraries to prevent the problem of theft, to modern databases like NoveList, which help solve the problem of what to read next. Professional practice in American librarianship has centered on problem solving from the beginning, from overarching problems like how to provide the best books to the most people at the lowest cost (put forth by Melvil Dewey in 1892 and still the motto of the ALA today)[11] to solving specific problems at local institutions, like how to increase circulation or teach information literacy.

---

11. http://www.ala.org/aboutala/missionpriorities

Like so many problems in design, the problems that libraries address can often be characterized as wicked. For example, let's look at contemporary online library catalogs. What is the exact definition of the problem these tools attempt to solve? Is it a question of material inventory, or information access? If it is access, is it ease of access, universality of access, remote access, or something else entirely? Perhaps the problem includes all of the above, as well as issues of integration with circulation and statistical reporting. It must also include the consideration of back-end architecture, display, descriptive cataloging, subject analysis, and authority control. Not only is the problem ill-defined and interconnected, but it also impacts a wide variety of stakeholders—library patrons, librarians, organizational management, and software vendors and developers. Even Patrick Wilson, the former professor and dean of the School of Information Studies at the University of California, Berkeley, writes that library catalogs are not faulty because of poor workmanship or outmoded organizational schemes, but rather due to a deeper inherent complexity.[12] It is exactly this kind of complexity that characterizes wicked problems.

Libraries can (and do) use *problem framing* to try to tackle these kinds of wicked problems, often by taking a particular perspective or view of a problem. For instance, the problem of accessing e-books in libraries can be reframed in various ways. How patrons find and download titles is very different from how library staff acquire those titles and make them accessible. How might we reframe this further? Viewing an issue from the point of view of both patrons and library staff is a common occurrence in library projects. What other views could we take on this

---

12. Patrick Wilson, *Two Kinds of Power: An Essay on Bibliographical Control* (Berkeley, CA: University of California Press, 1968).

issue? How about different types of patrons: adults, children, teens? How about different environments those patrons are in: the library, work, school, home, on the road commuting? Other methods for reframing problems include setting boundaries around the issue ("How do children use library e-books?"), selecting particular aspects of the problem to pay attention to ("How can we make the download process quick and easy?"), and imposing coherence ("What is the process children follow to find a library e-book?"). Libraries frequently draw upon problem framing in their work, even if they don't explicitly call it by that name or recognize it as a kind of design work.

And like other design fields, libraries *create* a range of tangible and intangible products to help address information problems. From the earliest libraries of Sumeria, where workers created cuneiform lists of holdings, to contemporary "book bikes"—bicycle-based mobile libraries—what separates a library from a mere collection is the creation of products, systems, and services that unite users with information. Some of these products may be physical, like the previous two examples. But other tools may be conceptual. For instance, the Dewey Decimal Classification is an intangible intellectual system of organization that enables patrons to browse shelves by discipline and subject. Other intangible products created by libraries include services like reference and readers' advisory, and programs like storytimes, ESL classes, and summer reading challenges. Although they are intangible themselves, many of these systems, programs, and services create tangible products as well, everything from policy documents and instruction manuals to marketing materials, all of which are created by library workers. These examples were chosen to illustrate the breadth and diversity of library design projects, and because many of them are likely to be familiar or recognizable, but for each project listed here there are hundreds of others, large and small, successes and failures. Arguably every tool, program, and service created in librarianship is a design product, from individual bibliographic records to cooperative reference service plans spanning large numbers of libraries.

Increasingly, libraries are not only creating their own tools and services, but are helping patrons and library users create their own tools and services to help themselves. This can clearly be seen in the increasing support for making within libraries. The rise of library makerspaces—areas and programs that allow patrons the opportunity to create intellectual and physical materials—has been a dramatic trend in the last fifteen years. Library makerspaces stem from an ethos of "learning by doing" and hands-on experience in creation, and makerspaces in the educational community at large have been explicitly recognized as a means to teach design thinking.[13] The growing presence of makerspaces and similar programs and services in libraries demonstrates their commitment to supporting patrons' applications of design thinking.

USER-CENTERED VS. HUMAN-CENTERED APPROACHES

Supporting patrons has always been a key component of librarianship, which has prided itself on being a *user-centered* profession. Early American librarianship was rooted in service to library users with the goal of improving their lives through exposure to books, reading, and literacy. Reading was emphasized as a means of intellectual, moral, and social education and improvement. But this meant that the tools and services created by libraries for users were often based less on what

---

13. For just a few examples, see http://www.makerspaceforeducation.com/design -thinking.html, https://www.getmagicbox.com/using-makerspaces-to-foster-design -thinking/, and http://renovatedlearning.com/2016/02/08/teaching-the-design-process/.

users *wanted* to read and more on what librarians thought users *should* read; usually this meant classic, culturally uplifting texts in the Western literary canon. Although this agenda certainly had users at its center, today it is criticized for its cultural presumption and its imposition of certain values.

Although the overarching goal of improving literacy still motivates the profession, the mid-twentieth century saw a turn away from *assumptions* about what users needed towards *investigations* of what users actually do need, or want. As education for librarianship became increasing situated in universities, an emphasis on scientific inquiry and evidence developed. Librarians began to use scientific methods to inform library decisions, increasingly using methods like surveys and interviews to assess users' wants and needs. In libraries, this has traditionally been referred to as "needs assessment." Librarians and library workers try to systematically uncover what needs patrons have, so they can focus on meeting and satisfying those needs. This truly goes to the service heart of librarianship and shows that the profession is indeed user-focused and service-oriented. Seminal theories like Ranganathan's famous Five Laws of Library Science (see figure 4) emphasize user-friendly libraries and collections. The ongoing interest in research about information-seeking and information behavior reflects a continuation of this theme, along with influences from user-centered design and UX fields, which have increasingly appeared in librarianship in recent years.

It's clear that libraries have always been user-centered. But although there is certainly overlap between the two approaches, being user-centered is not exactly the same as being *human-centered*. User-centered approaches, by their very name, focus on use: things like completing a task or accomplishing a goal. The word *user* reduces people to their use of a thing, rather than engaging with their experiences as human

FIGURE 4 ————————————————————————————————————
Ranganathan's Five Laws of Library Science

First law	Books are for use
Second law	Every reader their book
Third law	Every book its reader
Fourth law	Save the time of the reader
Fifth law	The library is a growing organism

beings. Traditional needs assessment tools, like surveys or interviews with users, can be helpful, but it is important to note their limitations. First, many of these assessments are still done within the context of preexisting tools and services (an assessment of what already exists and how it is—or isn't—being used), rather than being conducted with an eye for designing new solutions (discovering what might be possible). Needs assessment is often couched in library terms, and it tends to piggyback on existing technologies and designs: Should we adopt LibGuides? Should we implement Text-A-Librarian? These questions are not human-centered—they do not ask what problems the person experiences in the course of interacting with information. These kinds of questions are *use*-centered, because they focus on the *use* of a particular software or product. By contrast, empathetic techniques show us what it feels like to be that user during a particular task or experience. To be human-centered is to take a more holistic approach, and view users as not just entities completing a task, but as human beings experiencing problems.

To be human-centered also requires the consideration of actual people, not demographics or market segments. The people at any given library are unique. The term *public library user* encompasses a huge variety of people—men, women, children, high school students, urban teens, rural farmers, seniors, families, and everyone in between. *Academic library users* may be faculty, staff, students, researchers, large universities, small colleges, students with different majors and subject areas . . . and the list goes on, for every library and type of library. If librarians don't understand these actual human beings, then they cannot design tools and services to meet their needs. Acquiring generic preexisting tools may or may not be the best design solution for a given library—but how can we know if we don't understand our users? Additionally, librarians need to empathize with library users both inside and outside of the library environment in order to discover not just what problems they encounter when using the library, but what information problems they face in society at large. Libraries are poised as the organizations to tackle these challenges, but until librarians know, understand, and empathize with the problems people face, they cannot begin to design tools and services to support and improve their experiences.

Additionally, traditional user needs assessment tools like surveys and interviews rely on users telling us what they want. Why is this a problem, you may ask? Asking users to identify their own needs assumes that (1) users actually know what they need (which they may not) and (2) even if they do know at some visceral level what they need, they may not know how to articulate or express that need clearly. Asking users what they want presumes that users possess the answers to such questions— but often users cannot imagine new solutions to their problems.[14] This places the burden of innovation and ideation on the users while also

---

14. Zoltán Gócza offers a good compendium of resources discussing this issue in "Myth #21: People Can Tell You What They Want," http://uxmyths.com/post/746610684/myth-21-people-can-tell-you-what-they-want.

absolving the librarian of the need to proactively generate new ideas. In this case, anything is not possible—the only possibilities considered are those suggested by (potentially uninformed) users.

WORKING WITH CONSTRAINTS

Another barrier to adopting an "anything is possible" mindset in librarianship is that libraries are sometimes too quick to focus on *constraints* like a lack of money, time, or staff, which leads to eliminating possibilities before they have been explored and developed. And this makes sense, given the historical precedents of efficiency in the profession established by Dewey and others early on, as well as contemporary situations where libraries face budget cuts and staff reductions. But libraries may preliminarily curtail innovation by only generating ideas that are inexpensive or otherwise easy to implement. While reality will always impose some practical limitations, like funding availability or staff time, there is a time and a place for considering constraints in all projects. What separates design thinking from other approaches is that it also explicitly allows—nay, requires—times when those practical limitations are disregarded. Having a mindset of possibility does not mean that the impossible must be made manifest. Ideas that seem impossible during brainstorming often lead to other, more implementable ideas. Crazy ideas like "talking dragons delivering books to children" are fine, and even encouraged. We all know that this idea is impossible because dragons don't exist. But maybe it inspires a new idea about people dressed as dragons reading stories to children. These kinds of implementable ideas wouldn't have come about without making an outrageous stretch outside the realm of possible. Multiple studies show that flexibility, creativity, and innovation are increasingly important skills for librarians and library workers in the twenty-first century. Fiscal and other constraints will always factor into design—it's making sure they're factored in at the right phase that's important. Curtailing the "anything is possible" mindset preemptively prevents the kinds of divergent thinking that are necessary for harnessing these twenty-first-century skills.

I suspect that one reason why libraries are so focused on constraints is because they are faced with so many of them. But perhaps another reason is their concern for success and a *fear of failure.* Pressure from constraints may make it seem like a project has only one opportunity for implementation or one chance for success—a mindset that is in direct contradiction to design thinking's emphasis on *iteration.* Libraries have spent years creating evaluation metrics to demonstrate their success, from usage statistics that indicate access, availability, and satisfaction to information literacy assessments that reflect the success rates of instruction. These metrics can be useful, but like user needs assessment, they are not without issues. For instance, a library I worked at instituted a new program for checking out laptop computers in order to solve the problem of limited computer availability. In the first few months we noticed high circulation of the laptops, which the director interpreted as indicating the popularity, and therefore the success of the program, which the director then touted to higher-ups. But in reality the laptops' batteries only lasted a short time, meaning that patrons had to continually return dead computers and check out new ones, much to their frustration. In this case, the high circulation rates didn't reflect success at all. Thankfully, when we realized what was happening, we were able to iterate on the service—we began making laptop chargers available for checkout as well. Of course, this led to a problem with limited electrical outlet availability in the library space, which led to the need for subsequent problem solving.

What enabled us to iterate in our problem solving? It wasn't the evaluation metrics (although they did reveal unusual circulation patterns that caught our attention). Though it was not explicit at the time, *reflection* in the form of thought and discussion helped us understand what wasn't working and why. Reflection is a large part of understanding what works or does not work about a design. There may be no numbers or statistics attached to it, but design reflection still incorporates evaluative criteria. One type of design reflection focuses on identifying *rationale*: the idea that every design decision needs a justification. Reflecting on the rationale or reasoning for our decision-making reveals much about whether or not a design solution is working and why. For instance, I've asked a number of libraries why they use the Dewey Decimal System. The most common rationale is simply that "it's always been that way." Other libraries that use alternative systems have a rationale for why they switched to a BISAC-based classification system: "to put customers at ease and help them become more self-sufficient and comfortable using the library."[15] You may or may not agree with this reasoning—but agreement is not the point. The point is that these libraries had an explicit reason for doing what they did. Understanding how patrons felt about the Dewey system—that the classification numbers intimidated them and made them feel inferior—led to this design choice and being able to evaluate on the basis of that rationale helps to reveal whether or not their design is working.

---

15. Barbara Fister, "The Dewey Dilemma," *Library Journal* 134, no. 16 (2009): 22–25.

DESIGN THINKING FROM THE FIELD

IT'S CLEAR THAT DESIGN THINKING IS HIGHLY RELevant to librarianship. While I touched on some general examples in the previous chapter, in this chapter I want to focus on some concrete examples of design thinking as it is applied in libraries and librarianship. Some of these examples are *implicit* ones, drawing on a design thinking mindset even though they were not overtly referred to as design projects. Others draw on design thinking more intentionally, and *explicitly* use the process model of design thinking to guide the development of new library products and services.

IMPLICIT APPLICATIONS OF DESIGN THINKING

As previously noted, design thinking is not a new concept. Many aspects of design thinking have been used in American librarianship, even before it was known by that name. Numerous historical examples reflect the various tenets of design thinking even though they were never called out or explicitly acknowledged as design. One of my favorite historical examples is the development of *Poole's Index to Periodical Literature*, the first American library tool to provide subject access to the articles within periodicals. *Poole's Index* was a formative, significant work that (1) provided the first means of access to periodical content in American libraries, (2) influenced how and in what ways libraries index periodicals, and (3) is still in use today in various formats.

Poole's Index is a seminal example of a solution to a wicked problem: a unique, interconnected, and poorly defined problem that cannot be definitively described. Although some title and author indexes did exist by the mid-nineteenth century, finding periodical writings on a particular topic was impossible unless you already knew in which magazine or newspaper an article on that topic had appeared. To combat this problem, in 1848 William Frederick Poole, a student at Yale University, compiled a subject index for all of the periodicals held by the Library of the Brothers in Unity, a debating group at Yale. However, while this was useful in solving the problem of subject access to periodicals within that specific library, new problems arose from its creation. Other librarians who purchased this first edition of the *Index* for use in their libraries soon found that the holdings and the location information for the periodicals were local to Yale (so if their own library had other additional titles, the *Index* could not help them locate articles within those periodicals).

From his first edition on, Poole used problem framing to help guide his design work. He framed the problem of periodicals access in a very specific way by focusing on *subject* access. Poole also framed the problem by identifying an intended user base: the students who used his library. This made for a group of users with vastly different characteristics than, say, genteel ladies of the time. Poole explicitly directed volunteers to index only the articles of interest to the "general student."[16] But even he clarified his framing of that domain in a very specific way: "By 'general student' I mean the *very cultured* general student."[17]

The second edition of the *Index* in 1853 addressed a larger range of periodicals and used universal location information, but the unprecedented growth of periodical literature meant that even as this new edition was published, it was already out of date. New periodicals were appearing that covered previously unaddressed topics, increasing the diversity of subject coverage. Poole quickly became overwhelmed trying to index all of this material by himself with only one assistant. The problem of how periodical indexing could keep up with the explosive growth of periodical literature remained unaddressed for almost twenty years, until the first meeting of what would subsequently become the American Library Association in 1876, where a plan was devised to create a third edition of the *Index*. This would be a cooperative venture with indexing help from librarians across the country, and it included a plan for publishing regularly scheduled supplements to index recently published works.

It is this specific iteration of *Poole's Index* along with its subsequent supplements that comprise what we commonly think of as "Poole's Index" today. We don't typically think of the 1848 or 1853 editions, leaving them to function more as early prototypes and multiple design iterations that led to the *Index* as we now know it. When faced with a lack of financial support for compiling a third edition, Poole fronted his own money, demonstrating a willingness to take a risk, even though the project might fail. The work for the third edition took six years

---

16. Letter, W. F. Poole to Morrison (March 1, 1878), Box 4, Folder 20, W.L. Williamson - William F. Poole Research Papers.

17. Ibid., emphasis in original.

and harnessed the volunteer labor of librarians from throughout the United States and England. But still new problems arose, such as how to standardize forms of entry among more than fifty indexers. Other issues emerged over time, such as the limitations of publishing physical books and the transition to digital formats in the twentieth century. Like all wicked problems, there is no stopping rule—even today, libraries and other information providers struggle with providing access to periodicals, a problem that is interconnected with topics like models of publishing, content ownership questions, and intellectual content creation. *Poole's Index* is an example of design thinking that lies at the heart of American librarianship, setting precedents for the profession that continue to be influential today.

Another prime example of early design thinking is the Washington County (MD) Free Library (WCFL) book wagon, also known as America's first bookmobile. Bookmobiles may seem ubiquitous and commonplace in today's libraries, but prior to the twentieth century, this service model did not yet exist in American librarianship. When she was hired in 1901 as the inaugural WCFL librarian, Mary Lemist Titcomb, a forty-four-year-old librarian from New England, was tasked with solving a wicked problem indeed: how to serve the urban and rural patrons of the county equitably and raise the literacy and cultural level of the county. After iterating through multiple designs like remote branches and book deposit stations, Titcomb hit on the idea of a "book wagon"—a horse-drawn carriage that delivered library books directly to remote farms and homesteads. Such a design had never been imagined before. Although not explicitly referred to as a "design thinker," historians have noted Titcomb's user-centered attitude, and newspaper articles from the time consistently refer to her as "an innovator." Beyond the many WCFL programs and services she created, she was noted for designing and making all her own "wearables" and even designing the plans for her own home. Her designerly mindset—especially her refusal to be limited to the possible—led her to develop a variety of innovative library services over the course of her thirty-year career at the Washington County Free Library.

Neither of these examples, nor any other historical examples, are commonly referred to as design. This is not surprising. After all, "design thinking" as we now know it hadn't been articulated yet. A clear understanding and articulation of design thinking did not even begin until the 1960s, so it would be ludicrous to expect these early projects to contain explicit references to design. But it would also be faulty to assume that situations and contexts of the past did not include a design concept simply because the same words were not used to describe it then as are used today. And in fact, we see that this is the case for much of design in librarianship. Even today, there are abundant examples of library work that draw on design thinking even if they are not explicitly called by that name. One of my favorite examples is the "tough topics" handout and related media. Created in 2015 by Justin Azevedo, a branch supervisor at the Sacramento (CA) Public Library, the handout contains a list of sensitive subjects, such as abuse, depression, and sex, with their corresponding Dewey Decimal Classification numbers. (See figure 5.)

Azevedo had noticed that teen self-help books circulated strongly, but reference questions about topics like abuse, depression, and sex were rare. Putting himself in a teen's shoes, he thought that not only would asking an adult about these topics be embarrassing, but it could pose a real privacy or safety threat if asked aloud in public or discovered by parents in a browser history or cache. So Azevedo created a handout which listed the Dewey numbers for books on these and many other sensitive topics, so teenagers could conveniently find them on the shelves

FIGURE 5 ——————————————————————————————

Original version of the "tough topics" handout from Sacramento Public Library (Courtesy of Justin Azevedo)

TEENS: HELP YOURSELF

Look for these numbers on the shelves, and don't forget the adult nonfiction.
Try searching these keywords in teen fiction, too.

abuse/incest	362.76
abusive relationships	362.8
acne/skin care	616.53, 646.726
alcohol	362.292, 613.81
birth control	613.94
body changes/puberty	612.661
body image	616.852
bullying	302.34
cutting/self-harm	616.8582
date rape/acquaintance rape	362.883
dating/relationships	305.235, 306.73, 646.77
depression	616.8527, 616.85844
divorce	306.89
domestic violence	362.8292
drugs	362.29, 616.86
eating disorders	616.8526
health/hygiene	613.04243, 613.7043
lesbian/gay/bisexual/transgender	306.766
pregnancy	306.8743, 618.2
rape/sexual assault	362.883
self-esteem	305.235
sex	613.951
sexually transmitted diseases	616.951
suicide	362.28, 616.8527

For more privacy, use the self-checkout machines.

without seeking the assistance of a librarian. Even though the handout wasn't created through a formal design thinking process, it was arguably an empathic tool for teens that helped identify a problem and create a solution to address that problem. The "tough topics" handout is also a good example of how other forms of evaluation beyond traditional assessment metrics can demonstrate success. While traditional metrics like the increased circulation of self-help resources might imply the successful deployment of the new handout, in this case its reception and iterative adoption also reveal the quality of the design. More libraries than I can count have adopted this tool in their own settings. Some have iterated on the idea, making bookmarks, posters, or offering topics lists online. Some have added additional text, guiding patrons to use self-checkout machines for additional privacy, or supplying telephone numbers for emergency support hotlines. Although the original handout design targeted teens, I have seen iterations that focus on other communities, such as adults or senior citizens. Azevedo himself notes that the 2015 handout has gone through formatting updates and revisions, and was itself originally inspired by a conversation on the YALSA Young Adult Advisory Councils (YA-YAAC) listserv. Like the historical cases cited earlier in this chapter, this example was not explicitly called "design thinking," but it harnessed key elements of the design thinking mindset, fundamental design methods, and phases of the design thinking process, thus demonstrating the strong role that design thinking continues to play in library practice.

EXPLICIT APPLICATIONS OF DESIGN THINKING

In addition to all of this *implicit* design work, in recent years the *explicit* application of design thinking, especially the design thinking process, has become increasingly prominent in the library field. In the early

2000s Steven Bell, an academic librarian, began explicitly pointing out the similarities between design thinking and library work and calling for the application of the design thinking process in libraries. His book with John Shank, *Academic Librarianship by Design* (2007), is one of the first explicit discussions of applying design approaches to librarianship. Like many librarians of the time, Bell encouraged shifting the focus of libraries from creating access to resources to creating meaningful relationships with community members. He proposed that one way to differentiate libraries while building these relationships was to design great library user experiences.[18]

Many of the earliest *explicit* applications of design thinking involved library projects in what were considered traditional design domains. Probably the most common example is the architecture and interior design of new or remodeled libraries. When design is discussed in the context of librarianship, it is often relegated to architecture and space planning, such as *Library Journal's* annual Design Showcase, which highlights architectural and interior design prowess. Design thinking is often used to construct or reconceive library spaces, such as the remodeling project at the John A. Prior Health Sciences Library at Ohio State University. In this project, librarians explicitly drew on the design thinking process when planning a renovation of the physical library space. Library staff observed faculty members and staff at work in the library, and they noticed an increase in problem-based learning, original research, and collaborative projects, as well as the combined use of analog and digital tools, ranging from skeletal models to laptops and PDAs. They also watched where and for how long patrons waited for library assistance. In addition to observations, library staff solicited

---

18. Steven Bell, "Design Thinking for Better Libraries," *Information Outlook* 15, no. 6 (2011): 10–11.

direct feedback via informal surveys and oral and written suggestions. The staff's brainstorming solutions to the issues they identified ranged from roving reference service to library-produced podcasts. Ultimately, the team refined the possible solutions and implemented a single service point—the ASK desk, which serves as a one-stop shop for information, circulation, and computing services. However, the process did not end with implementation. True to the design thinking process, ongoing evaluation and investigation led to additions and revisions, such as downsizing the area for photocopying as the demand for that service ebbed, and increasing the availability of staff with copyright expertise in order to field the growing number of questions on that topic.

In another example, a team of library staff and design professionals used the design thinking process to create a new coworking space at the Bezazian Branch of the Chicago Public Library. (A coworking space is a flexible, multi-use office space that hosts independent, self-directed activities by work-at-home professionals, freelancers, and other adult workers who may be working for different organizations.) First, in the investigative phase, the team visited diverse examples of existing coworking spaces—many of them outside of library contexts. They interviewed users of those spaces in order to understand their needs and desires. They also interviewed library patrons for similar information. After synthesizing what they found out about people's coworking needs, they brainstormed ideas for coworking spaces in the library. Next, they created a prototype space in the library and observed how people used it. Aspects of the space that were not working were either modified or eliminated entirely and replaced with other approaches, thus beginning the cycle anew. New perspectives surfaced, such as the need to support job seekers. Additional coworking spaces as well as services to assist with employment will be developed based on what they learned from the original prototype. These projects reiterate the role of the library as a "third place" and acknowledge that these kinds of spaces do not just happen—they must be intentionally designed to be welcoming and to support the communities that visit them.

Although physical spaces lend themselves well to design thinking projects, Bell emphasizes that design thinking should be used to improve library experiences—both in terms of physical space and in terms of practices and services. At his own workplace, Temple University Libraries, Bell draws on design thinking to improve all manner of library experiences—everything from reducing the amount of time students wait for printing, to branding and marketing the library across campus. Other examples of library user experiences that have been improved with design thinking include signage and wayfinding at the University of Technology Sydney,[19] data management at Oklahoma State University,[20] and transfer student relations at the University of Washington.[21]

Projects like the eXtensible Catalog at the University of Rochester used design methods to understand what patrons really wanted from their libraries. Librarians at that university observed that students faced problems using the library catalog. To understand the frame and context of the problem, they brought in Nancy Fried Foster, an anthropologist,

19. Edward Luca and Bhuva Narayan, "Signage by Design: A Design-Thinking Approach to Library User Experience," *Weave: Journal of Library User Experience* 1, no. 5 (2016), http://dx.doi.org/10.3998/weave.12535642.0001.501.

20. Cynthia Ippoliti, "Research as Design, Design as Research: Applying Design Thinking to Data Management Needs Assessment," Proceedings of the 2016 Library Assessment Conference, http://old.libraryassessment.org/bm~doc/4-ippoliti-2016.pdf.

21. Linda Whang, Christine Tawatao, John Danneker, Jackie Belanger, Stephen Edward Weber, Linda Garcia, and Amelia Klaus, "Understanding the Transfer Student Experience Using Design Thinking," *Reference Services Review* 45, no. 2 (2017): 298–313, https://doi.org/10.1108/RSR-10-2016-0073.

for an investigative phase exploring exactly what, how, and why under-graduate students conducted research and scholarship. To generate ideas for solutions to the problem, the library held participatory design work-shops in which teams of students were asked to design an app that would assist them with group work. The ultimate goal of these workshops was not to build an app, but to generate ideas about what students needed to perform and complete their scholarly work: the librarians weren't interested in the app design itself, but instead in how the participants' app ideas revealed what kinds of work they needed to be able to do when conducting research or working on a course project. The knowledge gleaned from these design sessions revealed that students work with a variety of materials and sources, which led to the creation of a new metadata schema that allowed records for materials of various formats to be united together into one collection and seamless user interface, thereby enabling the students to search one location rather than multiple silos. In addition to using a design activity to uncover problems in an empathetic way, the eXtensible Catalog project also eschewed traditional assessment methods due to their lack of human-centeredness. Instead of surveys or interviews asking users what they might need to search for information, the team sat down with students and faculty and watched as they attempted to search for information in real time and in the con-text of a real-world research project or assignment. This allowed them to better understand the context in which problems occurred and gave them a better idea of what kinds of solutions might be useful.

Such approaches are not limited to academic libraries. As a frontrun-ner in the use of design thinking in libraries, I again look to the Chicago Public Library. One of my favorite examples is from a team working in the Literature and Language Department that wanted to better assist patrons who are interested in learning English. To understand what navigating the library might be like for a non-English-literate patron, the team took a trip to a local Korean grocery store. They brought a list of items to find, but the list was written in Korean—a language that none of the team members were able to speak or read. They declined to ask any of the grocery store's staff for assistance, in order to experience what it might be like to search for items in an unfamiliar language without help. Based on what they learned from this immersive empathetic experience, they reorganized their entire English Language Learners section and created signage in both English and the different languages of their patrons.

TOOLS AND SERVICES TO SUPPORT DESIGN THINKING

With the explicit application of design thinking on the rise in libraries, many tools and services to support design thinking in libraries are emerging. The best-known resource is probably Design Thinking for Libraries: A Toolkit for Patron-Centered Design (designthinkingforlibraries.com). This toolkit was developed by IDEO in partnership with the Chicago Public Library and the Aarhus Public Libraries in Denmark. With financial support from the Bill & Melinda Gates Foundation, the team observed more than forty librarians across ten countries to gather insights about ways that design thinking might be applicable to libraries. Libraries and librarians can use the resulting toolkit to learn what design thinking is and apply methods of design thinking to their work. The toolkit provides a step-by-step guide to adopting design thinking as a staff-driven process for change. The toolkit's popularity continues to contribute to greater awareness about design thinking among library workers.

In 2016 the Library Journal Design program, which initially focused on architectural challenges that united librarians and architects in exploring the use of design to improve library services, began to offer a design thinking workshop in conjunction with the Chicago Public Library. The Design Thinking for Libraries website is collecting examples of design thinking practice in libraries (http://designthinkingforlibraries.com/examples/). Other online tools, like the blogs at the Blended Librarians Online Learning Community (http://blendedlibrarian.org) and Designing Better Libraries (http://dbl.lishost.org) websites, offer practicing librarians opportunities to participate in discussions and information exchange. These contemporary examples are just a few select instances of libraries applying the design thinking process to improve library services. More examples are happening every day—maybe yours will be next!

FOR THE FUTURE

IT'S CLEAR THAT DESIGN THINKING IS INCREAS-
ingly relevant to libraries in the twenty-first century. But
what can we expect in the future? If we adhere to the design
thinking mindset, we know that design work is iterative
and never done, and so we should always be thinking about
what's next, what new problems are emerging and how we
might be able to address them. Although no one knows for
sure what the future holds, if libraries want to harness the
power of design thinking, they need to explicitly apply it
and be intentional in their design work. Librarians need to
acknowledge—and embrace—their roles as designers. In
this chapter I offer three overarching suggestions to help
librarians make this transition: (1) understand and apply
elements from the larger context of design, (2) evolve
from human-centered design to values-centered design,
and (3) include design explicitly in LIS education and
workplace culture.

THERE'S MORE TO DESIGN THAN DESIGN THINKING

Design thinking has certainly come under criticism for not being the magical panacea it is sometimes touted to be. In a scathing TED Talk, Natasha Jen even called it "bullsh*t," and just a meaningless buzzword. Design thinking has been criticized for being both too vague and too prescriptive; for focusing too much on impossibly lofty ideas without a consideration of real-world implementation needs; and for creating good ideas that still inevitably die in committee.

While no approach is without its flaws, most of these criticisms are ill-founded. They stem from a misunderstanding of what design thinking is, such as a limited view of design thinking solely as a magical step-by-step process: just follow the prescribed phases and ta-da, success! But no process works in a vacuum. You cannot expect to apply any process successfully without understanding and embracing the worldview that underlies it. That is why I am so keen to emphasize the dual nature of design thinking as *both process and mindset.* Once the mindset of design is taken into account, many of the typical criticisms fall flat. Understanding the mindset in more depth helps combat vague definitions and understandings of design thinking. A person with a thorough understanding of design knows that it is not solely about ideating impossible ideas—there is a time and a place to consider constraints, but it is important to make sure these are considered in the appropriate context and not preemptively. And those great design ideas that die in committee? Without support throughout an organization, no process can produce good results. That's not a fault of design thinking—that's a product of closed-minded organizational culture.

Other criticisms of design thinking hold more weight. Although design thinking is rooted in emulating the real work that designers do, it does not fully encompass all of the aspects of that work. No process model can capture all of the elements and nuances of a particular context. There is so much more to design than design thinking. Many people mistakenly consider design to be an applied field, a subset of art or science. But design is actually its own overarching discipline, at the same level as the sciences or the arts and humanities. Just as there are multiple fields within the discipline of science (biology, chemistry, etc.) that are united by overarching ideologies such as the scientific method, and multiple branches of the humanities (history, philosophy, etc.) united by perspectives of interpretation, design unites multiple fields (fashion design, product design, interior design, etc.) by fundamental disciplinary perspectives. I like to call this "big-D design" or "design writ large" in order to distinguish it from specific applications of design (fashion design, graphic design, etc.) or particular approaches to design (system-centered design, participatory design, etc.). It is this overarching discipline of design that lays the foundations for the design thinking mindset. However, crucial aspects that are prevalent in "design writ large" that span all these domains and approaches are at best implicit and at worst are missing entirely from design thinking.

One key element of design that's missing from the design thinking model is *critique*. Critique is a rigorous form of evaluation that is central to the discipline of design. Critique may call to mind scary memories of harsh, negative criticism, perhaps in front of peers, like reading a poem aloud in a creative writing class only to have the instructor and classmates rip it to shreds. However, well-executed design critique is not subjective negativity. Critique is not about whether you "like" a design or approve of its aesthetics. A good critique says *why* something does or does not work for that individual. It asks questions and helps elicit the rationale for a design decision. A critique is about discovering what's not working in order to make a design better. It can be a hard process to learn to take critique well, and even harder to learn to give a critique well. The critique of a design—especially one you are emotionally invested in—can feel like a personal blow. This is why it's important to seek critique throughout the design process—if ideas are just sketches, disposable and without investment, then critique of them becomes easier and can also be incorporated into new sketches, thus continuing the cycle. And although other forms of evaluation are built into the design thinking process, such as user feedback and testing, established structures of critique from mentors and peers are not. A constructive critique of library work, from both our patrons and our peers, could be a useful and insightful means of evaluation and feedback. Critique sessions at conferences like the American Library Association's annual meeting would not only offer the benefits of direct feedback to participants, but would also authoritatively endorse design methods and thinking as valid approaches to librarianship.

Another central tenet of design write large that is conspicuously absent from the design thinking model is *reflection*. Many of us are familiar with reflection, the process in which we look back on a completed project or past situation with serious thought and consideration. There are myriad examples of reflection in librarianship, from teaching (such as Char Booth's book *Reflective Teaching, Effective Learning: Instructional Literacy for Library Educators* [2011]) to storytimes (such as VIEWS 2, a research project which found purposeful reflection to be a key component in the continuous improvement of storytimes intended to increase literacy skills). Libraries are well-positioned to integrate their reflective capacity, yet there is no space provided for explicit reflection in the design thinking process. While reflection might be referenced cursorily in the evaluative phase, to harness the power of this process it needs to be intentional, with time set aside for it and other commitments to the process that demonstrate its value.

Some of the hardest aspects of design to accomplish, such as critique and reflection, are things I think we need to see more of—and more support for—in our profession. Making use of these and other additional aspects of design writ large, rather than just limiting ourselves to design thinking, will help libraries create improved tools and services in the future.

FROM HUMAN-CENTERED DESIGN TO VALUES-CENTERED DESIGN

Other, more substantive critiques of design thinking have focused on its reduction to a process model. Bruce Nussbaum, a professor of innovation and design at the Parsons School of Design and author of *Creative Intelligence* (2013), says that "Design Thinking has given the design profession and society at large all the benefits it has to offer and is beginning to ossify and actually do harm."[22] While he advocates for a new consideration of "creative intelligence" to help combat these harms, I think future libraries can use design to prevent and even heal harms in society, by connecting with their already existing commitment to a set of core professional values (figure 6).

As previously noted, there are many different design approaches. Librarianship is still evolving from a user-centered perspective to a

---

22. Bruce Nussbaum, "Design Thinking Is a Failed Experiment. So What's Next?" *Fast Company*, April 5, 2011, https://www.fastcompany.com/1663558/design-thinking -is-a-failed-experiment-so-whats-next.

FIGURE 6 ——

Core values of librarianship

Access	The Public Good
Confidentiality/Privacy	Preservation
Democracy	Professionalism
Diversity	Service
Education and Lifelong Learning	Social Responsibility
Intellectual Freedom	Sustainability

From http://www.ala.org/advocacy/intfreedom/corevalues.

human-centered perspective, which accordingly influences the field's approach to design. Moving from more traditional user needs assessment strategies that focus on usage and task completion to more empathetic understanding of users' library and information experiences is a major perspective shift. Design thinking, with its heavy reliance on human-centered design, can and has helped with this positive turn. But it is increasingly clear that while beneficial, even human-centered empathy is not enough.

Dr. Katherine Crocker, a public health researcher at Columbia University, notes that too much focus on empathy can be problematic. The purpose of empathy, she argues, is to facilitate coalition-building and finding common ground, but there are some values so abhorrent that they should defy cooperation. She uses the example of fascism, noting that to empathize with fascist principles leads to cooperation with fascist principles, ultimately lending support to fascism. The goals of seeking a cooperative common ground are evident in librarianship's traditional notions of neutrality and objectivity. Yet libraries are not and never have been neutral. Explicitly articulating a set of values clearly indicates non-neutral positioning. Taking positions to support things like access, literacy, diversity, and intellectual freedom cannot be a neutral or objective standpoint. While design is always about solving problems, Jeanne Liedtka notes that design is about more than just what solutions are possible: that design is about what *could* be or arguably what *should* be.[23] The former merely identifies options, while the latter makes a judgment about the world. Librarianship takes the position not just that people *could* have access to resources, but that they *should;* not just that intellectual freedom is possible, but that it is beneficial, both to individuals and to society at large. This also means that libraries need to look beyond library users as their sole design audience. Libraries are in service to their users and local communities, but as social institutions they are also in service to society at large. Libraries of the future need to start recognizing and acknowledging society as its own form of design client. Instead of asking design questions like "How might we reduce computer waiting times for our students?" or "How might we improve the English language skills of refugees in our community?" libraries of the future need to start asking bigger questions that tackle the wicked problems of society, like "How might we encourage more people to read?"

Values and perspectives about how the world "should" be are embodied in library artifacts regardless of libraries' neutral intentions. Because all design products are created by human beings, human values are embedded in them, whether on purpose or unintentionally. One famous

---

23. Jeanne Liedtka, "Design Thinking: The Role of Hypothesis Generation and Testing," in *Managing as Designing*, ed. R. J. Boland and F. Collopy (Stanford, CA: Stanford University Press, 2004).

example is the overpass bridges designed by Robert Moses on the Southern State Parkway, which offered access from Queens to eastern Long Island in New York. Moses intentionally designed bridges with a low clearance, so low that buses could not pass underneath them. This prevented those who relied on buses for public transportation—notably poor Black and Puerto Rican people—from reaching Jones Beach, a popular summer recreation area. While this example of the embedding of racist values in architectural design may seem like history, there are plenty of contemporary examples. Safiya Umoja Noble's book *Algorithms of Oppression* (2018) is notable for demonstrating racism and bias in the algorithms used in search engines. Regardless of intention, the values of any design's creators become entrenched in their creations. As bastions of values such as access, literacy, diversity, and intellectual freedom, libraries need to proactively ensure that these positive values are the ones embedded in library tools and services. For example, one of these core values is a commitment to protect and maintain patrons' privacy. This may have been easy in a paper-based world where librarians declined to share circulation records. And certainly many of today's libraries have policies in place that prevent employees from revealing patrons' personal and circulation data. But in today's digital world, libraries increasingly rely on digital products from vendors and other external sources to keep track of patron information. Do you know what the privacy policies are for your ILS? If you are not the person or team designing that product, do you have any control over how that patron data is stored or used? It is designers, not users, who have the power to control what values become embedded in design products. As libraries increasingly face competition and constraints from other information service providers like Google and Wikipedia, what makes—and keeps—libraries unique is a set of core professional values.

THE INTENTIONAL EMBRACE OF DESIGN

To achieve these goals and ensure that library values are not compromised, librarians need to take control of library designs. The only way to accomplish this is for librarians to *acknowledge and own their identities and roles as designers*. This may be hard for a profession that has positioned itself as a social science for almost 100 years. For instance, even though there has been an increase in the number of library UX positions in recent years, these positions are often staffed by non-librarians. Additionally, the work of these roles usually focuses on the user research portion of the design process, while any actual creation and implementation are handed off to other staff, like information technology employees or consultants. But as librarianship is increasingly viewed as a design profession, librarians need to reclaim their rightful roles as creators, not just clients.

I see two major areas that can help shift this identity. The first is rooted in *education* for librarianship. Design needs to be a major component of future graduate-level library education programs (e.g., MLIS programs). While some programs already include assignments based on design thinking within individual classes, or even offer entire courses on the topic, programs need to teach more than just the design thinking process model if they want to foster graduates who are collaborative, creative, socially innovative, flexible, and adaptable problem solvers—all characteristics specifically identified as necessary for future library professionals.[24] Programs need to embrace design holistically, and reframe the profession as a design profession, rather than a social science. Increasing

---

24. John C. Bertot, Lindsay C. Sarin, and Johnna Percell, "Re-Envisioning the MLS: Findings, Issues, and Considerations," College of Information Studies, University of Maryland, College Park, 2015, http://mls.umd.edu/wp-content/uploads/2015/08/ReEnvisioningFinalReport.pdf.

diversity in MLIS programs will also foster empathy among students and facilitate the diverse collaborative teams needed for innovative idea generation. While "diversity" in the context of MLIS programs usually refers to people of different ethnic and racial backgrounds, design teams have seen proven benefit from bringing together people of various educational backgrounds and subject specialties, a practice that MLIS programs and librarianship are well-positioned to support. However, the number of students entering MLIS programs with design education backgrounds is disproportionately low, so perhaps programs could benefit from recruiting people who are already familiar with and practiced in design thinking.

Formal library education is also a space where future librarians can learn to embrace failure. A recent forum sponsored by the Institute of Museum and Library Services brought together MLIS educators and library practitioners to discuss design thinking in library education. One consistent theme was a strong fear of failure among contemporary MLIS students, which is a significant detriment to a design mindset. To combat this, educators need to help students see that their graduate education is not a high-pressure, one-shot opportunity. Instead, it is just one small part of a design repertoire that students can proactively build, just as designers build their knowledge repertoire from any and all past experiences—previous projects (both failures and successes), the projects of others, client discussions, and even personal experiences like watching movies or viewing art.

In addition to formal education, *organizational culture* also plays a significant role in reshaping identity. Many libraries already integrate some aspects of design thinking, but these are often underground, implicit, and unsupported. We need buy-in and support from the top: from local library management all the way up to the American Library

Association. It's not enough for ALA and other organizations to spread the word—they too must adopt design methods and approaches to serve as examples. Libraries want increasingly innovative staff, yet the organizations themselves are not set up to support models of thought that power innovation.

As previously noted, many design projects have failed not because they were inherently poor products, but from a lack of organizational support. Sometimes the remedy for this can be as easy as hiring people who already have a design mindset—people with design backgrounds or who have worked on design projects at other libraries. Another option is to adopt design thinking from within: we can use existing resources and exercises (such as the Design Thinking for Libraries Toolkit) to get started with the design mindset. I know it can be hard to institute these kinds of changes—especially ones that hinge on failure, iteration, and the idea that work is never done—especially when reporting to larger entities that seem to only care about successful finished products. But just as librarians need to defend other unique aspects of their profession, they also need to advocate for design culture in the same way. How much will financial or circulation numbers matter when your library is downsized or closed because it's doing the same-old-same-old, offering services that people can get elsewhere? You can use design to show how your library differs from other information services, especially in relation to the values of librarianship.

Physical and emotional environments also play a significant role in supporting and encouraging design thinking. A supportive team is helpful, and many libraries should be commended for their collegial staff and productive interactions, but if even the best team is cordoned off into cubicles or separate spaces, the possibilities for collaboration diminish. Designers need some sort of shared space in which to exchange ideas. A regularly scheduled meeting is the typical library approach, but there is something missing here. Design studios offer a permanent space where designers can tack up and share ideas, their work in progress, and other materials. This not only creates an immersive environment of constant exposure, it also helps inspire ideas on the fly rather than being forced to think about the project or brainstorm in a pre-specified time slot. I don't know of anyone who has ideas or inspiration on a set schedule; many people are inspired by other information and materials to which they are exposed. It is the responsibility of library managers and directors to create and support a design-friendly and encouraging "studio." This does not require a complete spatial revamp. Even small, integrated setups like a dedicated wall or bulletin board for ideas can help foster an environment that encourages and inspires design.

To conclude, there are two possible futures for libraries: one is a passive future, in which libraries sit back and let others design solutions to information problems. The second one, and the one I know I prefer, is the one that libraries design. Design thinking is so pervasive in librarianship that libraries and librarians already have the power to create unique, powerful, value-laden experiences and help individuals, communities, and even societies solve information problems. It's time to embrace design as a fundamental component of librarianship in order to create a better future for all.

SELECTED RESOURCES

ONLINE RESOURCES

IDEO. *Design Thinking for Libraries: A Toolkit for Patron-Centered Design.*
　　Palo Alto: IDEO, 2015. http://designthinkingforlibraries.com/.
"A Virtual Crash Course in Design Thinking." d.school, Hasso Plattner Insti-
　　tute of Design at Stanford University. http://dschool.stanford.edu/dgift/.

Note that there are other useful resources from both IDEO and Stanford
d.school throughout their websites.

FOUNDATIONAL READINGS ON DESIGN

There has been so much written on design that it's difficult to narrow it
down to a few suggestions. The following resources represent well-known
scholarly works that guide the idea of design as a unique discipline,
with a distinct philosophy and worldview that informs how knowledge
is created. Presented in chronological order, the resources below can
get you started; the references and citations in each of these works will
offer additional resources.

Simon, Herbert. *The Sciences of the Artificial, Third Edition*. Cambridge, MA: MIT Press, 1969.

Simon was one of the first scholars to write about design as a distinct worldview; he explored design in terms of problem solving via artifact creation. However, much of his work is an attempt to understand design in a scientific way. Future scholars, such as Schön and Cross (referenced below), explore how looking at design from only this perspective can be limiting.

Rittel, Horst, and Melvin Webber. "Dilemmas in a General Theory of Planning." *Policy Sciences* 4, no. 2(1973): 155–169.

This piece is the first to introduce the concept and definition of wicked problems.

Winner, Langdon. "Do Artifacts Have Politics?" *Daedalus* 109, no. 1 (1980): 121–136.

This is a famous article demonstrating the lack of neutrality in design artifacts and how design products reflect values, either implicitly or explicitly. The example of Robert Moses' bridge designs comes from this article.

Schön, Donald. *The Reflective Practitioner*. New York: Basic Books, 1983.

This resource is one of many early studies to observe and analyze what actually occurs during the design process; Schön's work is considered fundamental in the design field.

Norman, Donald A. *The Design of Everyday Things*. New York: Basic Books, 2002.

This book has helped shift the field to a user-centered design perspective and is well-known for its readability and accessibility to the layperson.

Cross, Nigel. *Design Thinking*. Oxford: Berg, 2011.

This work is one of many pieces Cross has written about design as a distinct worldview that emerges from what he calls "designerly ways of knowing." I suggest this one because it draws on and synthesizes many of his earlier writings as well as writings of others.

Nelson, Harold, and Erik Stolterman, *The Design Way*. Cambridge, MA: MIT Press, 2012.

A more modern take on design philosophy and ways of knowing, this book discusses how service is integral to design. Much of the viewpoints shared in this resource are easily visible in librarianship, making it a useful resource.

READINGS ON DESIGN IN LIBRARIANSHIP

An increasing number of pieces are being written on the intersection of design and libraries. These range from practical, how-to type articles to theoretical arguments about the role of design in librarianship. Here are some selected examples that span this range.

Bell, Steven J. "Design Thinking." *American Libraries* 39 no. 1/2 (2008): 44–49.

Braun, Linda. "Using Design Thinking: Providing a Framework for Youth Activities." *American Libraries* 47, no. 6 (2016): 80.

Clark, Jason A. "Anticipatory Design: Improving Search UX Using Query Analysis and Machine Cues." *Weave: Journal of Library User Experience* 1, no. 4 (2016).

Clarke, Rachel Ivy. "Designing a New Librarianship." *Journal of New Librarianship* 2, no. 2 (2017). https://www.newlibs.org/article/3144-designing-a-new-librarianship.

Clarke, Rachel Ivy. "Toward a Design Epistemology for Librarianship." *The Library Quarterly: Information, Community, Policy* 88, no. 1 (2018): 41–59.

Clarke, Rachel Ivy. "The Role of Design in *Poole's Index to Periodical Literature*: Implications for American Librarianship." *Libraries: Culture, History, Society* 3, no. 2 (2019): 129–154.

Clarke, Rachel Ivy, Satyen Amonkar, and Ann Rosenblad. "Design Thinking and Methods in Library Practice and Graduate Library Education." *Journal of Librarianship and Information Science* (September 2019). https://doi.org/10.1177/0961000619871989.

Marquez, Joe, and Annie Downey. "Service Design: An Introduction to a Holistic Assessment Methodology of Library Services." *Weave: Journal of Library User Experience* 1, no. 2 (2015): 1–16.

Mills, J. Elizabeth, Kathleen Campana, and Rachel Ivy Clarke. "Learning by Design: Creating Knowledge Through Library Storytime Production." In *Proceedings of the 79th Annual Meeting of the American Society for Information Science and Technology* 53, no. 1 (2016): 1–6.

Public Library Association. "Designing Spaces for People, Not Collections." November 2, 2016. Archived webinar. http://www.ala.org/pla/education/onlinelearning/webinars/ondemand/pla2016rewind/spaces.

Subramaniam, Mega. "Designing the Library of the Future for and with Teens: Librarians as the 'Connector' in Connected Learning." *Journal of Research on Libraries and Young Adults* 7, no. 2 (2016).

DESIGN METHODS AND TECHNIQUES

Carroll, Antionette. "Diversity & Inclusion in Design: Why Do They Matter?" AIGA, July 1, 2014. https://www.aiga.org/diversity-and -inclusion-in-design-why-do-they-matter.

"Design Method Toolkit." Digital Society School, Amsterdam University of Applied Sciences. https://toolkits.dss.cloud/design/

Martin, Bella, & Bruce Hanington. *Universal Methods of Design: 100 Ways to Research Complex Problems, Develop Innovative Ideas, and Design Effective Solutions*. Beverly, MA: Rockport Publishers, 2012.

Parker, Jake. "Finished Not Perfect." Video. *YouTube*, August 30, 2016. https://www.youtube.com/watch?v=lRtV-ugIT0k.

Stickdorn, Marc, and Jakob Schneider. *This Is Service Design Thinking: Basics—Tools—Cases*. Amsterdam: Bis Publishers, 2012.

Stickdorn, Marc, Markus Edgar Hormess, Adam Lawrence, and Jakob Schneider. *This Is Service Design Methods: A Companion to This Is Service Design Doing: Expanded Service Design Thinking Methods for Real Projects*, 1st ed. Sebastopol, CA: O'Reilly Media, Inc, 2018.

Value Sensitive Design Research Lab. http://vsdesign.org.
    Various writings and tools can be found on this website.